POPULAR SONGS
HAL LEONARD STUDENT PIANO LIBRARY

INTERMEDIATE

HIP-HOP
FOR PIANO SOLO

10 INVENTIVE ARRANGEMENTS

BY LOGAN EVAN THOMAS

T0079347

ISBN 978-1-70512-510-6

For all works contained herein:
Unauthorized copying, arranging, adapting, recording, internet posting, public performance,
or other distribution of the music in this publication is an infringement of copyright.
Infringers are liable under the law.

Visit Hal Leonard Online at
www.halleonard.com

Contact us:
Hal Leonard
7777 West Bluemound Road
Milwaukee, WI 53213
Email: info@halleonard.com

In Europe, contact:
Hal Leonard Europe Limited
42 Wigmore Street
Marylebone, London, W1U 2RN
Email: info@halleonardeurope.com

In Australia, contact:
Hal Leonard Australia Pty. Ltd.
4 Lentara Court
Cheltenham, Victoria, 3192 Australia
Email: info@halleonard.com.au

FROM THE ARRANGER

Ever since the birth of hip-hop, the infectious beats, hooks, and rhymes from so many artists and producers have tremendously shaped our culture and society. Ultimately, hip-hop is a "feeling." Traditionally, the core of the music was based on a four- or eight-measure drum loop and chopped up harmonic and melodic samples, which can often be difficult to capture on the piano... until now.

My goal with this book was to capture the essence of that "feeling" in a slick and clever pianistic way that is fun to play, constantly engaging, and performance ready. The only challenge you will have will be to stay on your piano bench, as this book will have your head nodding and body moving while you play through 10 of the most iconic hip-hop songs of our time! I sincerely hope you enjoy playing these arrangements as much as I had fun creating them. May you get the "feeling."

Logan Evan Thomas
February 2021

CONTENTS

Can't Hold Us

Words and Music by Raymond Dalton,
Ben Haggerty and Ryan Lewis
Arranged by Logan Evan Thomas

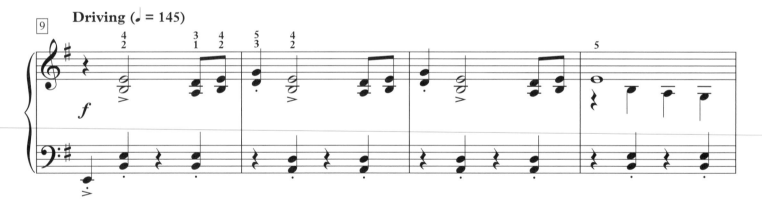

Copyright © 2011 MRL Entertainment, Macklemore LLC and Ryan Lewis Publishing
All Rights Administered by Songs Of Kobalt Music Publishing
All Rights Reserved   Used by Permission

Family Business

Words and Music by
Kanye West
Arranged by Logan Evan Thomas

Laid-back Hip-hop groove (♩ = 94)

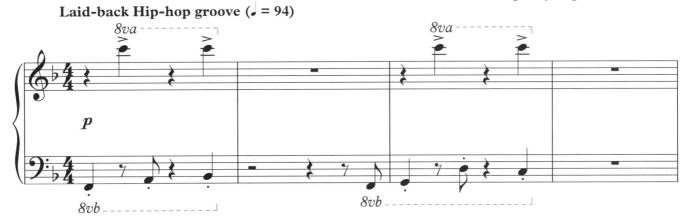

Copyright © 2004 EMI Blackwood Music Inc. and Please Gimme My Publishing, Inc.
All Rights Administered by Sony/ATV Music Publishing LLC, 424 Church Street, Suite 1200, Nashville, TN 37219
International Copyright Secured   All Rights Reserved

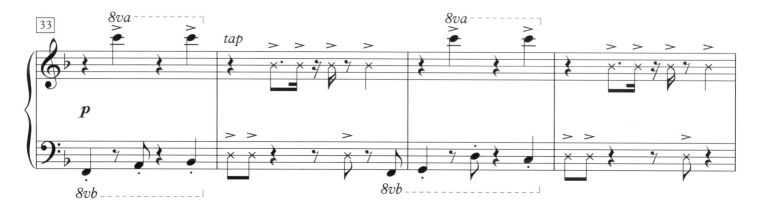

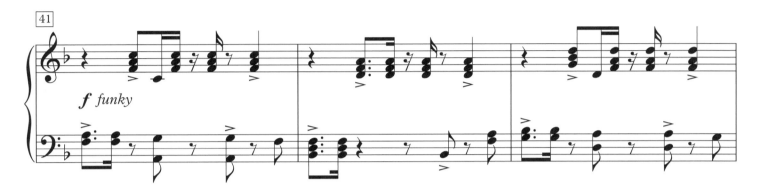

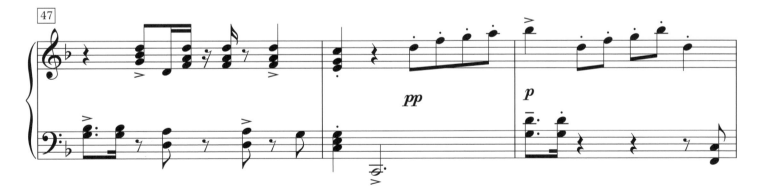

Empire State of Mind

Words and Music by Alicia Keys,
Shawn Carter, Jane't Sewell,
Angela Hunte, Al Shuckburgh,
Bert Keyes and Sylvia Robinson
Arranged by Logan Evan Thomas

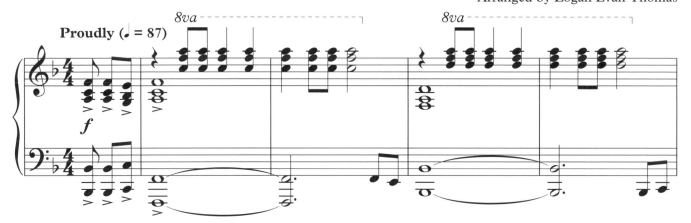

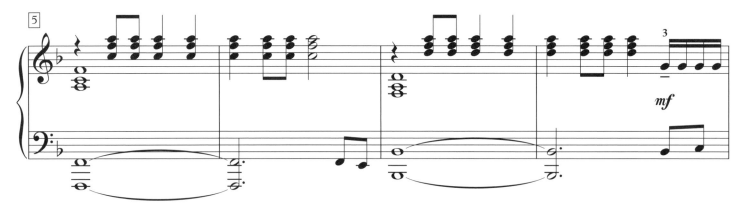

Copyright © 2009 EMI April Music Inc., EMI Foray Music, Lellow Productions, Masani Elshabazz Music,
J Sewell Publishing, Global Talent Publishing, Twenty Nine Black Music, WC Music Corp. and Carter Boys Music
All Rights on behalf of EMI April Music Inc., EMI Foray Music, Lellow Productions and Masani Elshabazz Music Administered by
Sony/ATV Music Publishing LLC, 424 Church Street, Suite 1200, Nashville, TN 37219
All Rights on behalf of Global Talent Publishing in the U.S. and Canada Administered by House Of Global Entertainment
All Rights on behalf of Carter Boys Music Administered by WC Music Corp.
International Copyright Secured   Used by Permission
- contains elements of "Love On A Two Way Street" (Keyes/Robinson) © 1970 Twenty Nine Black Music and Gambi Music Inc.

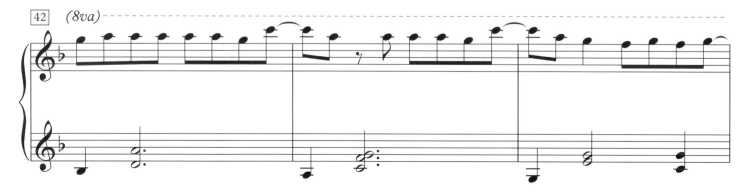

Hotline Bling

Words and Music by Aubrey Graham,
Paul Jefferies and Timmy Thomas
Arranged by Logan Evan Thomas

Playful (♩ = 135)

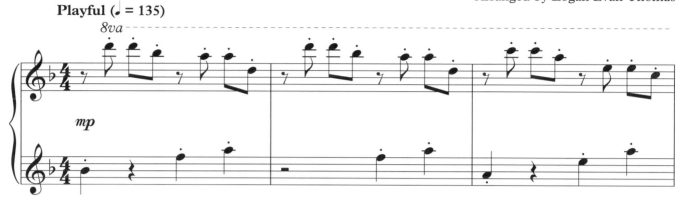

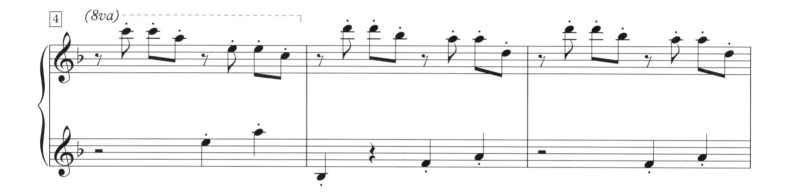

Copyright © 2015 EMI April Music Inc., EMI Music Publishing Ltd., Nyankingmusic and EMI Longitude Music
All Rights Administered by Sony/ATV Music Publishing LLC, 424 Church Street, Suite 1200, Nashville, TN 37219
International Copyright Secured   All Rights Reserved

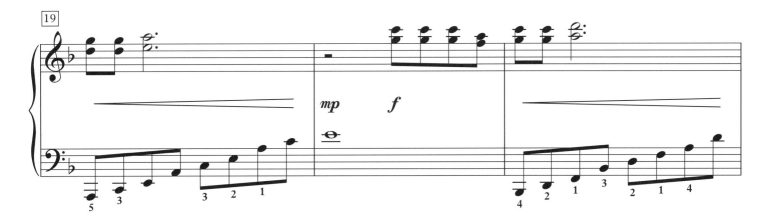

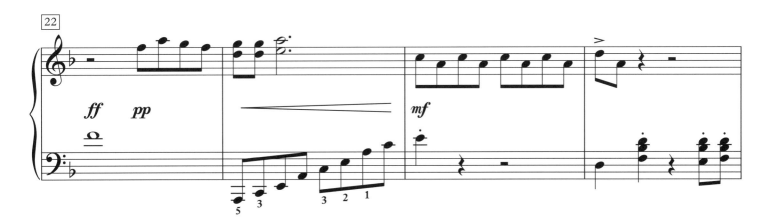

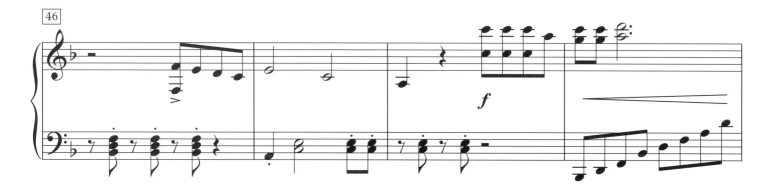

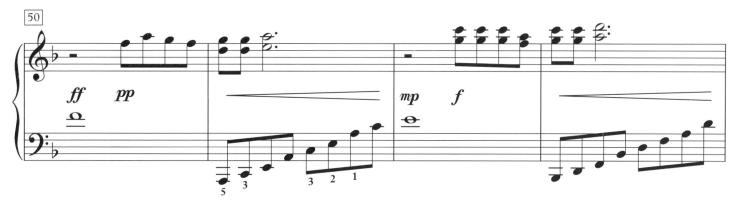

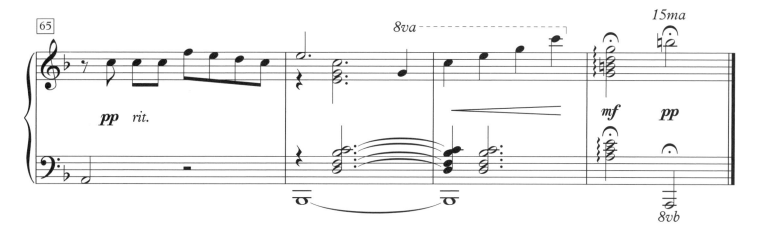

Love the Way You Lie

Words and Music by Alexander Grant,
Marshall Mathers and Holly Haferman
Arranged by Logan Evan Thomas

Somber (♩ = 87)

Copyright © 2010 SONGS OF UNIVERSAL, INC., SHROOM SHADY MUSIC, UNIVERSAL MUSIC - Z SONGS, HOTEL BRAVO MUSIC and M SHOP PUBLISHING
All Rights for SHROOM SHADY MUSIC Controlled and Administered by SONGS OF UNIVERSAL, INC.
All Rights for HOTEL BRAVO MUSIC and M SHOP PUBLISHING Controlled and Administered by UNIVERSAL MUSIC - Z SONGS
All Rights Reserved   Used by Permission

Hip-Hop groove

★ *opt. gliss. with palm*

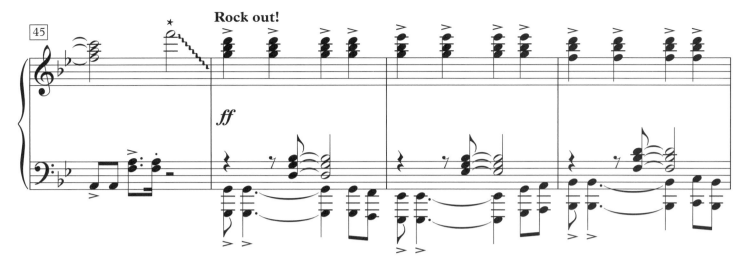

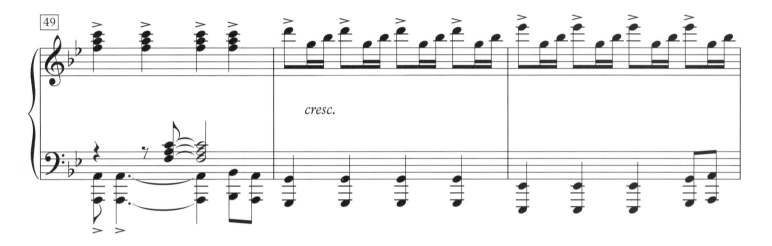

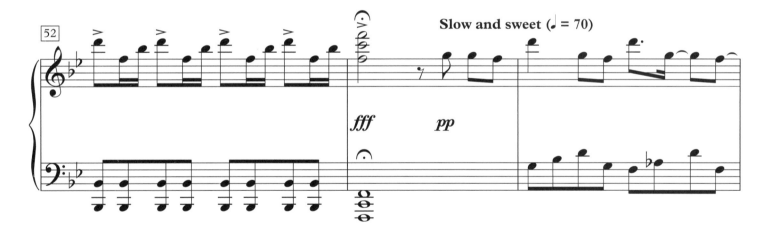

* opt. glissando

Ms. Jackson

Words and Music by David Sheats,
Andre Benjamin and Antwan Patton
Arranged by Logan Evan Thomas

Steady (♩ = 94)

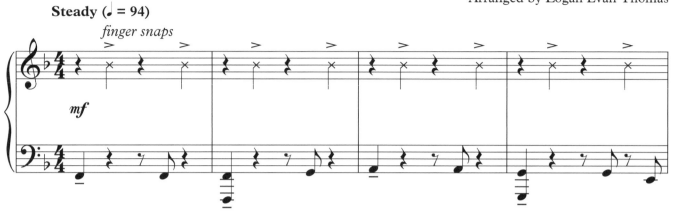

Copyright © 2000 EMI April Music Inc., Dungeon Rat Music and Gnat Booty Music
All Rights on behalf of EMI April Music Inc. and Dungeon Rat Music Administered by Sony/ATV Music Publishing LLC, 424 Church Street, Suite 1200, Nashville, TN 37219
All Rights on behalf of Gnat Booty Music Administered by BMG Rights Management (US) LLC
International Copyright Secured   All Rights Reserved

Sweetly

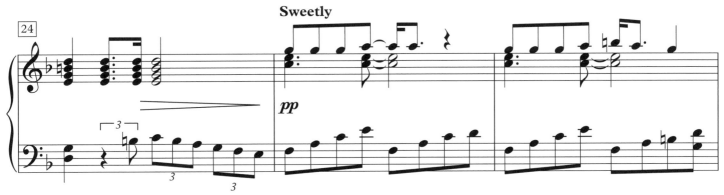

Old Town Road
(I Got The Horses in the Back)

Words and Music by Trent Reznor,
Atticus Ross, Kiowa Roukema
and Montero Lamar Hill
Arranged by Logan Evan Thomas

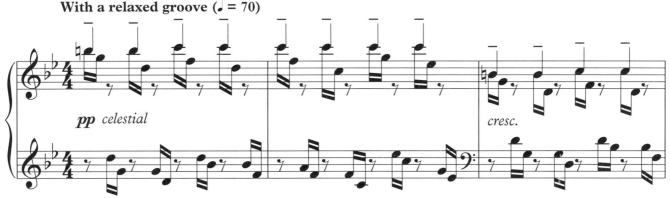

Copyright © 2019 Form And Texture, Inc., Songs In The Key Of Mink, Young Kio Publishing and Sony/ATV Music Publishing LLC
All Rights for Form And Texture, Inc. Administered Worldwide by Kobalt Songs Music Publishing
All Rights for Songs In The Key Of Mink and Young Kio Publishing Administered by Songs Of Universal, Inc.
All Rights for Sony/ATV Music Publishing LLC Administered by Sony/ATV Music Publishing LLC, 424 Church Street, Suite 1200, Nashville, TN 37219
All Rights Reserved   Used by Permission
- Incorporates the song "34 Ghosts IV" (Words and Music by Atticus Ross and Trent Reznor)

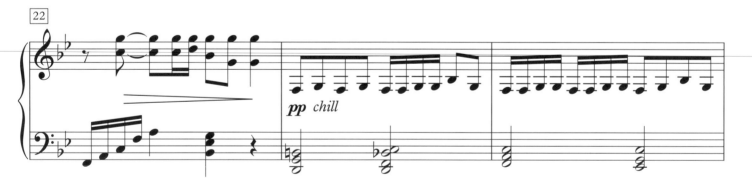

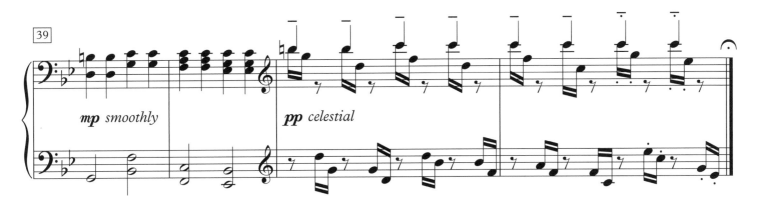

Sunday Candy

Words and Music by Nico Segal,
Greg Landfair, Jr., Nate Fox,
Marvin Winans, Jamila Woods,
Peter Wilkins, Chancelor Bennett
and Jabari Rayford
Arranged by Logan Evan Thomas

Copyright © 2014 Painted Desert Music Corp., Ultra International Music Publishing LLC, Stixjams Publishing, Seven Peaks Music, All Day Recess,
The Real Brain Publishing, Crouch Music, Bud John Songs, Blk Girl Art, Real Cottontale Music, Chancelor Bennett Publishing Designee and Rayford Music Publishing
All Rights for Painted Desert Music Corp. Administered by Reservoir Media Management, Inc.
All Rights for Ultra International Music Publishing LLC and Stixjams Publishing in the U.S. and Canada Administered by Ultra Empire Music
All Rights for All Day Recess and The Real Brain Publishing Administered by Seven Peaks Music
All Rights for Crouch Music and Bud John Songs Administered at CapitolCMGPublishing.com
All Rights for Blk Girl Art Administered Worldwide by Kobalt Group Publishing
All Rights for Real Cottontale Music Administered Worldwide by Kobalt Songs Music Publishing
All Rights Reserved   Used by Permission

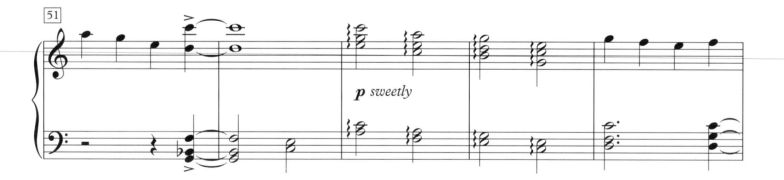

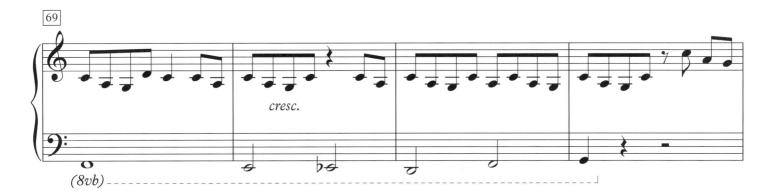

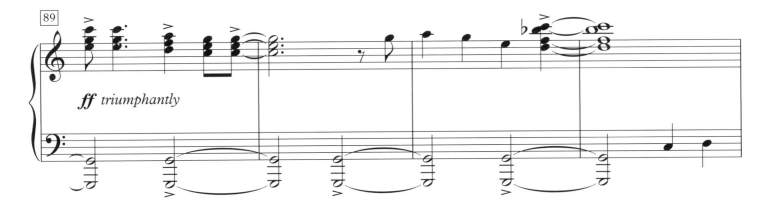

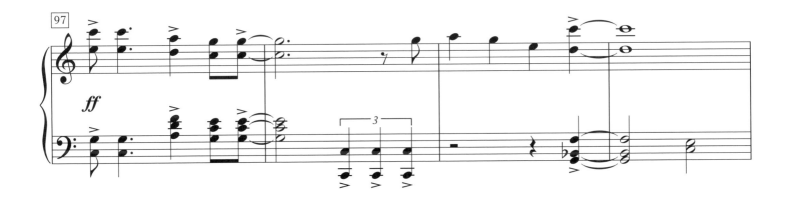

Sunflower

from SPIDER-MAN: INTO THE SPIDER-VERSE

Words and Music by Austin Richard Post,
Carl Austin Rosen, Khalif Brown,
Carter Lang, Louis Bell and Billy Walsh
Arranged by Logan Evan Thomas

Relaxed, not too fast (♩ = 88)

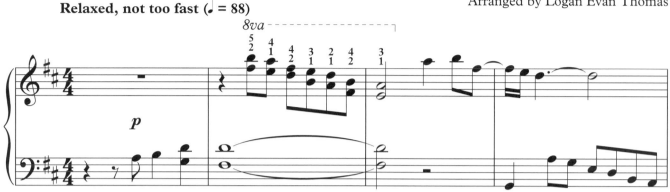

Copyright © 2018 SONGS OF UNIVERSAL, INC., POSTY PUBLISHING, ELECTRIC FEEL MUSIC, WARNER-TAMERLANE PUBLISHING CORP.,
KHALIF BROWN BMI PUB DESIGNEE, EARDRUMMERS ENTERTAINMENT LLC, WC MUSIC CORP., CARTER LANG PUB DESIGNEE, ZUMA TUNA LLC,
EMI APRIL MUSIC INC., NYANKINGMUSIC, WMMW PUBLISHING, TWENTY FIFTEEN BOULEVARD MUSIC INC. and TWENTY FIFTEEN AVENUE MUSIC INC.
All Rights for POSTY PUBLISHING and ELECTRIC FEEL MUSIC Administered by SONGS OF UNIVERSAL, INC.
All Rights for KHALIF BROWN BMI PUB DESIGNEE and EARDRUMMERS ENTERTAINMENT LLC Administered by WARNER-TAMERLANE PUBLISHING CORP.
All Rights for CARTER LANG PUB DESIGNEE and ZUMA TUNA LLC Administered by WC MUSIC CORP.
All Rights for EMI APRIL MUSIC INC., NYANKINGMUSIC, WMMW PUBLISHING, TWENTY FIFTEEN BOULEVARD MUSIC INC.
and TWENTY FIFTEEN AVENUE MUSIC INC. Administered by SONY/ATV MUSIC PUBLISHING LLC, 424 Church Street, Suite 1200, Nashville, TN 37219
All Rights Reserved   Used by Permission

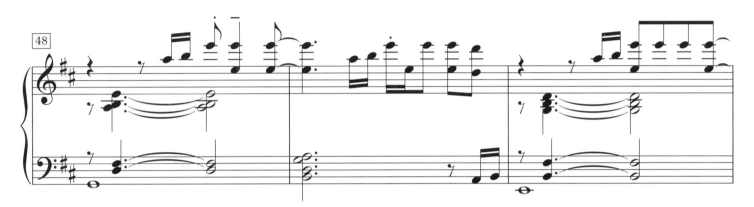

Super Bass

Words and Music by Onika Maraj,
Roahn Hylton, Esther Dean,
Daniel Johnson and Jeremy Coleman
Arranged by Logan Evan Thomas

With a chill vibe (♩ = 126)

Copyright © 2011 MONEY MACK MUSIC, HARAJUKU BARBIE MUSIC, EMI APRIL MUSIC INC., FB DA MASTERMIND MUSIC PUBLISHING, PEERMUSIC III LTD.,
DAT DAMN DEAN MUSIC, ARTIST 101 PUBLISHING GROUP, IN THE BUILDING MUSIC PUBLISHING, ARTIST PUBLISHING GROUP WEST and JMIKEMUSIC
All Rights for MONEY MACK MUSIC and HARAJUKU BARBIE MUSIC Administered by SONGS OF UNIVERSAL, INC.
All Rights for EMI APRIL MUSIC INC. and FB DA MASTERMIND MUSIC PUBLISHING Administered by
SONY/ATV MUSIC PUBLISHING LLC, 424 Church Street, Suite 1200, Nashville, TN 37219
All Rights for DAT DAMN DEAN MUSIC Administered by PEERMUSIC III LTD.
All Rights for ARTIST 101 PUBLISHING GROUP and IN THE BUILDING MUSIC PUBLISHING Administered Worldwide by SONGS OF KOBALT MUSIC PUBLISHING
All Rights for ARTIST PUBLISHING GROUP WEST and JMIKEMUSIC Administered Worldwide by KOBALT SONGS MUSIC PUBLISHING
All Rights Reserved   Used by Permission

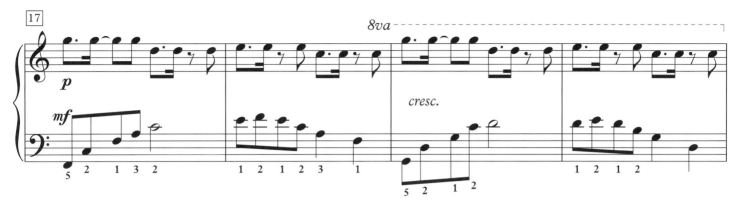

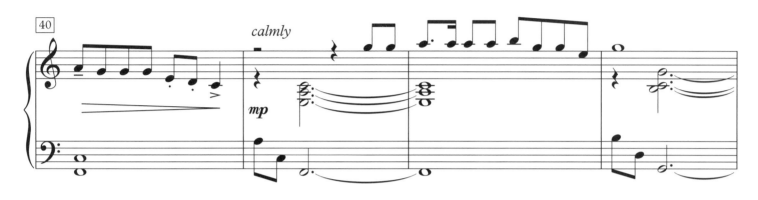

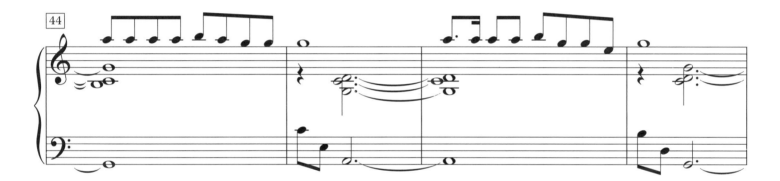

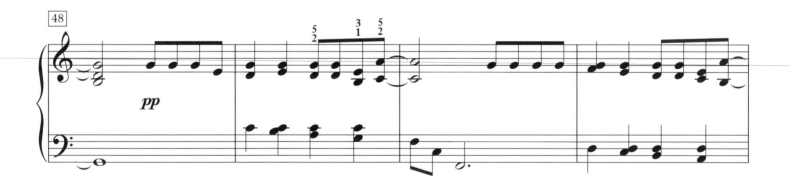

POPULAR SONGS
HAL LEONARD STUDENT PIANO LIBRARY

The **Hal Leonard Student Piano Library** has great songs, and you will find all your favorites here: Disney classics, Broadway and movie favorites, and today's top hits. These graded collections are skillfully and imaginatively arranged for students and pianists at every level, from elementary solos with teacher accompaniments to sophisticated piano solos for the advancing pianist.

Adele
arr. Mona Rejino
Correlates with HLSPL Level 5
00159590.............................$12.99

The Beatles
arr. Eugénie Rocherolle
Correlates with HLSPL Level 5
00296649.............................. $12.99

Irving Berlin Piano Duos
arr. Don Heitler and Jim Lyke
Correlates with HLSPL Level 5
00296838.............................$14.99

Broadway Favorites
arr. Phillip Keveren
Correlates with HLSPL Level 4
00279192.............................$12.99

Chart Hits
arr. Mona Rejino
Correlates with HLSPL Level 5
00296710.................................$8.99

Christmas at the Piano
arr. Lynda Lybeck-Robinson
Correlates with HLSPL Level 4
00298194.............................$12.99

Christmas Cheer
arr. Phillip Keveren
Correlates with HLSPL Level 4
00296616...............................$8.99

Classic Christmas Favorites
arr. Jennifer & Mike Watts
Correlates with HLSPL Level 5
00129582.................................$9.99

Christmas Time Is Here
arr. Eugénie Rocherolle
Correlates with HLSPL Level 5
00296614.................................$8.99

Classic Joplin Rags
arr. Fred Kern
Correlates with HLSPL Level 5
00296743.................................$9.99

Classical Pop – Lady Gaga Fugue & Other Pop Hits
arr. Giovanni Dettori
Correlates with HLSPL Level 5
00296921.............................$12.99

Contemporary Movie Hits
arr. by Carol Klose, Jennifer Linn and Wendy Stevens
Correlates with HLSPL Level 5
00296780.................................$8.99

Contemporary Pop Hits
arr. Wendy Stevens
Correlates with HLSPL Level 3
00296836.................................$8.99

Cool Pop
arr. Mona Rejino
Correlates with HLSPL Level 5
00360103.............................$12.99

Country Favorites
arr. Mona Rejino
Correlates with HLSPL Level 5
00296861.................................$9.99

Disney Favorites
arr. Phillip Keveren
Correlates with HLSPL Levels 3/4
00296647.............................$10.99

Disney Film Favorites
arr. Mona Rejino
Correlates with HLSPL Level 5
00296809 ....$10.99

Disney Piano Duets
arr. Jennifer & Mike Watts
Correlates with HLSPL Level 5
00113759.............................$13.99

Double Agent! Piano Duets
arr. Jeremy Siskind
Correlates with HLSPL Level 5
00121595.............................$12.99

Easy Christmas Duets
arr. Mona Rejino & Phillip Keveren
Correlates with HLSPL Levels 3/4
00237139.................................$9.99

Easy Disney Duets
arr. Jennifer and Mike Watts
Correlates with HLSPL Level 4
00243727.............................$12.99

Four Hands on Broadway
arr. Fred Kern
Correlates with HLSPL Level 5
00146177.............................$12.99

Frozen Piano Duets
arr. Mona Rejino
Correlates with HLSPL Levels 3/4
00144294.............................$12.99

Hip-Hop for Piano Solo
arr. Logan Evan Thomas
Correlates with HLSPL Level 5
00360950.............................$12.99

Jazz Hits for Piano Duet
arr. Jeremy Siskind
Correlates with HLSPL Level 5
00143248.............................$12.99

Elton John
arr. Carol Klose
Correlates with HLSPL Level 5
00296721.............................$10.99

Joplin Ragtime Duets
arr. Fred Kern
Correlates with HLSPL Level 5
00296771.................................$8.99

Movie Blockbusters
arr. Mona Rejino
Correlates with HLSPL Level 5
00232850.............................$10.99

The Nutcracker Suite
arr. Lynda Lybeck-Robinson
Correlates with HLSPL Levels 3/4
00147906.................................$8.99

Pop Hits for Piano Duet
arr. Jeremy Siskind
Correlates with HLSPL Level 5
00224734.............................$12.99

Sing to the King
arr. Phillip Keveren
Correlates with HLSPL Level 5
00296808.................................$8.99

Smash Hits
arr. Mona Rejino
Correlates with HLSPL Level 5
00284841.............................$10.99

Spooky Halloween Tunes
arr. Fred Kern
Correlates with HLSPL Levels 3/4
00121550.................................$9.99

Today's Hits
arr. Mona Rejino
Correlates with HLSPL Level 5
00296646.................................$9.99

Top Hits
arr. Jennifer and Mike Watts
Correlates with HLSPL Level 5
00296894.............................$10.99

Top Piano Ballads
arr. Jennifer Watts
Correlates with HLSPL Level 5
00197926.............................$10.99

Video Game Hits
arr. Mona Rejino
Correlates with HLSPL Level 4
00300310.............................$12.99

You Raise Me Up
arr. Deborah Brady
Correlates with HLSPL Level 2/3
00296576.............................$7.95

HAL•LEONARD®
7777 W. BLUEMOUND RD. P.O. BOX 13819 MILWAUKEE, WI 53213

Prices, contents and availability subject to change without notice. Prices may vary outside the U.S.

Visit our website at www.halleonard.com

COMPOSER SHOWCASE
HAL LEONARD STUDENT PIANO LIBRARY

This series showcases great original piano music from our **Hal Leonard Student Piano Library** family of composers. Carefully graded for easy selection.

BILL BOYD

JAZZ BITS (AND PIECES)
Early Intermediate Level
00290312 11 Solos......................$7.99

JAZZ DELIGHTS
Intermediate Level
00240435 11 Solos......................$8.99

JAZZ FEST
Intermediate Level
00240436 10 Solos......................$8.99

JAZZ PRELIMS
Early Elementary Level
00290032 12 Solos......................$7.99

JAZZ SKETCHES
Intermediate Level
00220001 8 Solos......................$8.99

JAZZ STARTERS
Elementary Level
00290425 10 Solos......................$8.99

JAZZ STARTERS II
Late Elementary Level
00290434 11 Solos......................$7.99

JAZZ STARTERS III
Late Elementary Level
00290465 12 Solos......................$8.99

THINK JAZZ!
Early Intermediate Level
00290417 Method Book............$12.99

TONY CARAMIA

JAZZ MOODS
Intermediate Level
00296728 8 Solos......................$6.95

SUITE DREAMS
Intermediate Level
00296775 4 Solos......................$6.99

SONDRA CLARK

DAKOTA DAYS
Intermediate Level
00296521 5 Solos......................$6.95

FLORIDA FANTASY SUITE
Intermediate Level
00296766 3 Duets......................$7.95

THREE ODD METERS
Intermediate Level
00296472 3 Duets......................$6.95

MATTHEW EDWARDS

CONCERTO FOR YOUNG PIANISTS
FOR 2 PIANOS, FOUR HANDS
Intermediate Level Book/CD
00296356 3 Movements $19.99

CONCERTO NO. 2 IN G MAJOR
FOR 2 PIANOS, 4 HANDS
Intermediate Level Book/CD
00296670 3 Movements............$17.99

PHILLIP KEVEREN

MOUSE ON A MIRROR
Late Elementary Level
00296361 5 Solos......................$8.99

MUSICAL MOODS
Elementary/Late Elementary Level
00296714 7 Solos......................$6.99

SHIFTY-EYED BLUES
Late Elementary Level
00296374 5 Solos......................$7.99

CAROL KLOSE

THE BEST OF CAROL KLOSE
Early to Late Intermediate Level
00146151 15 Solos..................$12.99

CORAL REEF SUITE
Late Elementary Level
00296354 7 Solos......................$7.50

DESERT SUITE
Intermediate Level
00296667 6 Solos......................$7.99

FANCIFUL WALTZES
Early Intermediate Level
00296473 5 Solos......................$7.95

GARDEN TREASURES
Late Intermediate Level
00296787 5 Solos......................$8.50

ROMANTIC EXPRESSIONS
Intermediate to Late Intermediate Level
00296923 5 Solos......................$8.99

WATERCOLOR MINIATURES
Early Intermediate Level
00296848 7 Solos......................$7.99

JENNIFER LINN

AMERICAN IMPRESSIONS
Intermediate Level
00296471 6 Solos......................$8.99

ANIMALS HAVE FEELINGS TOO
Early Elementary/Elementary Level
00147789 8 Solos......................$8.99

AU CHOCOLAT
Late Elementary/Early Intermediate Level
00298110 7 Solos......................$8.99

CHRISTMAS IMPRESSIONS
Intermediate Level
00296706 8 Solos......................$8.99

JUST PINK
Elementary Level
00296722 9 Solos......................$8.99

LES PETITES IMAGES
Late Elementary Level
00296664 7 Solos......................$8.99

LES PETITES IMPRESSIONS
Intermediate Level
00296355 6 Solos......................$8.99

REFLECTIONS
Late Intermediate Level
00296843 5 Solos......................$8.99

TALES OF MYSTERY
Intermediate Level
00296769 6 Solos......................$8.99

LYNDA LYBECK-ROBINSON

ALASKA SKETCHES
Early Intermediate Level
00119637 8 Solos......................$8.99

AN AWESOME ADVENTURE
Late Elementary Level
00137563 8 Solos......................$7.99

FOR THE BIRDS
Early Intermediate/Intermediate Level
00237078 9 Solos......................$8.99

WHISPERING WOODS
Late Elementary Level
00275905 9 Solos......................$8.99

MONA REJINO

CIRCUS SUITE
Late Elementary Level
00296665 5 Solos......................$8.99

COLOR WHEEL
Early Intermediate Level
00201951 6 Solos......................$9.99

IMPRESIONES DE ESPAÑA
Intermediate Level
00337520 6 Solos......................$8.99

IMPRESSIONS OF NEW YORK
Intermediate Level
00364212......................$8.99

JUST FOR KIDS
Elementary Level
00296840 8 Solos......................$7.99

MERRY CHRISTMAS MEDLEYS
Intermediate Level
00296799 5 Solos......................$8.99

MINIATURES IN STYLE
Intermediate Level
00148088 6 Solos......................$8.99

PORTRAITS IN STYLE
Early Intermediate Level
00296507 6 Solos......................$8.99

EUGÉNIE ROCHEROLLE

CELEBRATION SUITE
Intermediate Level
00152724 3 Duets......................$8.99

ENCANTOS ESPAÑOLES (SPANISH DELIGHTS)
Intermediate Level
00125451 6 Solos......................$8.99

JAMBALAYA
Intermediate Level
00296654 2 Pianos, 8 Hands.....$12.99
00296725 2 Pianos, 4 Hands.......$7.95

JEROME KERN CLASSICS
Intermediate Level
00296577 10 Solos......................$12.99

LITTLE BLUES CONCERTO
Early Intermediate Level
00142801 2 Pianos, 4 Hands......$12.99

TOUR FOR TWO
Late Elementary Level
00296832 6 Duets......................$9.99

TREASURES
Late Elementary/Early Intermediate Level
00296924 7 Solos......................$8.99

JEREMY SISKIND

BIG APPLE JAZZ
Intermediate Level
00278209 8 Solos......................$8.99

MYTHS AND MONSTERS
Late Elementary/Early Intermediate Level
00148148 9 Solos......................$8.99

CHRISTOS TSITSAROS

DANCES FROM AROUND THE WORLD
Early Intermediate Level
00296688 7 Solos......................$8.99

FIVE SUMMER PIECES
Late Intermediate/Advanced Level
00361235 5 Solos......................$12.99

LYRIC BALLADS
Intermediate/Late Intermediate Level
00102404 6 Solos......................$8.99

POETIC MOMENTS
Intermediate Level
00296403 8 Solos......................$8.99

SEA DIARY
Early Intermediate Level
00253486 9 Solos......................$8.99

SONATINA HUMORESQUE
Late Intermediate Level
00296772 3 Movements.............$6.99

SONGS WITHOUT WORDS
Intermediate Level
00296506 9 Solos......................$9.99

THREE PRELUDES
Early Advanced Level
00130747 3 Solos......................$8.99

THROUGHOUT THE YEAR
Late Elementary Level
00296723 12 Duets....................$6.95

ADDITIONAL COLLECTIONS

AT THE LAKE
by Elvina Pearce
Elementary/Late Elementary Level
00131642 10 Solos and Duets.....$7.99

CHRISTMAS FOR TWO
by Dan Fox
Early Intermediate Level
00290069 13 Duets....................$8.99

CHRISTMAS JAZZ
by Mike Springer
Intermediate Level
00296525 6 Solos......................$8.99

COUNTY RAGTIME FESTIVAL
by Fred Kern
Intermediate Level
00296882 7 Solos......................$7.99

LITTLE JAZZERS
by Jennifer Watts
Elementary/Late Elementary Level
00154573 9 Solos......................$8.99

PLAY THE BLUES!
by Luann Carman
Early Intermediate Level
00296357 10 Solos......................$9.99

ROLLER COASTERS & RIDES
by Jennifer & Mike Watts
Intermediate Level
00131144 8 Duets......................$8.99

 HAL•LEONARD®

www.halleonard.com

Prices, contents, and availability subject to change without notice.

FOLK SONG SERIES

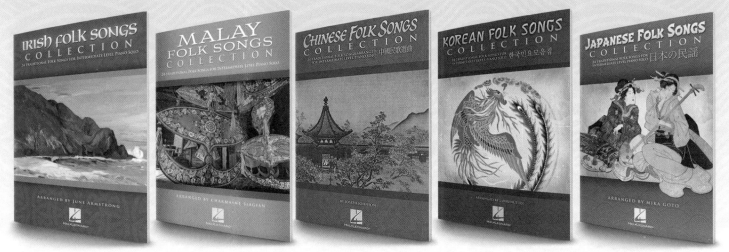

Introduce piano students to the music of world cultures with these folk songs arranged for intermediate piano solo. Each collection features 24 folk songs and includes detailed notes about the folk songs, beautiful illustrations, as well as a map of the regions.

AFRICAN AMERICAN FOLK SONGS COLLECTION
24 TRADITIONAL FOLK SONGS FOR
INTERMEDIATE LEVEL PIANO SOLO | arr. Artina McCain
The Bamboula • By and By • Deep River • Didn't My Lord Deliver Daniel? • Don't You Let Nobody Turn You Around • Every Time I Feel the Spirit • Give Me That Old Time Religion • Guide My Feet • I Want Jesus to Walk With Me • I Was Way Down A-Yonder • I'm a Soldier, Let Me Ride • In Bright Mansions Above • Lift Ev'ry Voice and Sing • Little David, Play on Your Harp • My Lord, What a Morning • Ride On, King Jesus • Run Mary Run • Sometimes I Feel Like a Motherless Child • Song of Conquest • Take Nabandji • Wade in the Water • Warriors' Song • Watch and Pray • What a Beautiful City.
00358084 Piano Solo...$10.99

IRISH FOLK SONGS COLLECTION
24 TRADITIONAL FOLK SONGS FOR
INTERMEDIATE LEVEL PIANO SOLO | arr. June Armstrong
As I Walked Out One Morning • Ballinderry • Blind Mary • Bunclody • Carrickfergus • The Castle of Dromore (The October Winds) • The Cliffs of Doneen • The Coolin • Courtin' in the Kitchen • Down Among the Ditches O • Down by the Salley Gardens • The Fairy Woman of Lough Leane • Follow Me Up to Carlow • The Gartan Mother's Lullaby • Huish the Cat • I'll Tell My Ma • Kitty of Coleraine • The Londonderry Air • My Lagan Love • My Love Is an Arbutus • Rocky Road to Dublin • Slieve Gallion Braes • Squire Parsons • That Night in Bethlehem.
00234359 Piano Solo...$9.99

MALAY FOLK SONGS COLLECTION
24 TRADITIONAL SONGS ARRANGED FOR
INTERMEDIATE LEVEL PIANO SOLO | arr. Charmaine Siagian
At Dawn • Chan Mali Chan • C'mon, Mama! • The Cockatoo • The Curvy Water Spinach Stalk • Five Little Chicks • God Bless the Sultan • The Goodbye Song • Great Indonesia • It's All Good Here • The Jumping Frog • Longing • Mak Inang • Milk Coffee • The Moon Kite • Morning Tide • My Country • Onward Singapore • Ponyfish • Song for the Ladybugs • The Stork Song • Suriram • Trek Tek Tek • Voyage of the Sampan.
00288420 Piano Solo...$10.99

CHINESE FOLK SONGS COLLECTION
24 TRADITIONAL SONGS ARRANGED FOR
INTERMEDIATE LEVEL PIANO SOLO | arr. Joseph Johnson
Beating the Wild Hog • Blue Flower • Carrying Song • Crescent Moon • Darkening Sky • Digging for Potatoes • Girl's Lament • Great Wall • Hand Drum Song • Homesick • Jasmine Flower Song • Little Cowherd • Love Song of the Prarie • Memorial • Mountaintop View • Northwest Rains • Running Horse Mountain • Sad, Rainy Day • Song of the Clown • The Sun Came Up Happy • Wa-Ha-Ha • Wedding Veil • White Flower • Woven Basket.
00296764 Piano Solo...$9.99

KOREAN FOLK SONGS COLLECTION
24 TRADITIONAL FOLK SONGS FOR
INTERMEDIATE LEVEL PIANO SOLO | arr. Lawrence Lee
Arirang • Autumn in the City • Birdie, Birdie • Boat Song • Catch the Tail • Chestnut • Cricket • Dance in the Moonlight • Five Hundred Years • Flowers • Fun Is Here • The Gate • Han River • Harvest • Jindo Field Song • Lullaby • The Mill • The Palace • The Pier • Three-Way Junction • Waterfall • Wild Herbs • Yearning • You and I.
00296810 Piano Solo...$9.99

JAPANESE FOLK SONGS COLLECTION
24 TRADITIONAL FOLK SONGS FOR
INTERMEDIATE LEVEL PIANO SOLO | arr. Mika Goto
Blooming Flowers • Come Here, Fireflies • Counting Game • The Fisherman's Song • Going to the Shrine • Harvest Song • Itsuki Lullaby • Joyful Doll Festival • Kimigayo • Let's Sing • My Hometown • Picking Tea Leaves • The Rabbit on the Moon • Rain • Rain Showers • Rock-Paper-Scissors • Sakura • Seven Baby Crows • Takeda Lullaby • Time to Go Home • Village Festival • Where Are You From? • Wish I Could Go • You're It!
00296891 Piano Solo...$9.99

HAL•LEONARD®
halleonard.com

Prices, contents and availability subject to change without notice.

LOGAN EVAN THOMAS is an award-winning pianist, composer, and producer residing in New York City. He has worked with Jennifer Lopez and Stefon Harris, and he currently tours as the pianist for Postmodern Jukebox. He has released three studio albums, two albums with his group Manner Effect, and has produced over 10 albums for artists of multiple genres. In 2010 he won 1st place at the Nottingham International Jazz Piano Competition and finished 2nd at the Montreux International Jazz Piano Competition. He was also a featured artist at the Gilmore International Keyboard Festival. As a composer, Thomas scored "A View from Sunset Park," winner of Best Documentary at the New York International Film Festival.